EGO LAND

by Jason

BALBOA.
PRESS

A DIVISION OF HAY HOUSE

Balboa Press books may be ordered through booksellers or by contacting:

Balboa Press
A Division of Hay House
1663 Liberty Drive
Bloomington, IN 47403
www.balboapress.com
1-(877) 407-4847

Because of the dynamic nature of the Internet, any Web addresses or links contained in this book may have changed since publication and may no longer be valid. The views expressed in this work are solely those of the author and do not necessarily reflect the views of the publisher, and the publisher hereby disclaims any responsibility for them.

The author of this book does not dispense medical advice or prescribe the use of any technique as a form of treatment for physical, emotional, or medical problems without the advice of a physician, either directly or indirectly. The intent of the author is only to offer information of a general nature to help you in your quest for emotional and spiritual well-being. In the event you use any of the information in this book for yourself, which is your constitutional right, the author and the publisher assume no responsibility for your actions.

Any people depicted in stock imagery provided by Thinkstock are models, and such images are being used for illustrative purposes only.
Certain stock imagery © Thinkstock.

ISBN: 978-1-4525-0066-9 (sc)
ISBN: 978-1-4525-0068-3 (dj)
ISBN: 978-1-4525-0067-6 (e)

Library of Congress Control Number: 2010914756

Printed in the United States of America

Balboa Press rev. date: 10/18/2010

This book is dedicated to my wonderful wife Lindsay who thru this whole process was strong enough to allow me the space to do this self inquiry.

I also have written this for my 2 wonderful sons to give them a guide line in their life, something to comfort them when they start to believe too much into their story.

Question:

What has you looking in books, joining classes, listening to CD's and going to spiritual teachers?

What are you really looking for?

I believe you are looking for YOU!!

"An awakened being intuitively knows the truth in a situation and will follow their life's purpose to raise the vibration of the planet and advance human consciousness"
(Unknown Author)

First off I would like to start of by saying thank you for having an open mind, for being flexible with your thinking and purchasing my book. I am not here to change your mind about anything you are experiencing but we will be discussing a lot of different topics concerning some things that may shock you and may upset you.

I suggest taking what resonates with you at this time and leave the rest as you may not be ready for it.

Please keep in mind that fear of something is what keeps you away from your unlimited power. So however you are evaluating your life at this time, I am here to share with you my experience. I am not a teacher, guru or someone that is enlightened.

"To observe without interference is true mastery."
(Unknown Author)

I believe we are already enlightened. You just need to remember who you are. Whatever path you are on all paths lead you back home and some are short and some are the long way.

When your foundation is rocked you will get angry, upset and you may even want to leave the room or burn this book. I call this the opening or the defensive action your EGO will take to protect itself.

The stuff that I will be discussing will empower and show you how you have been disempowered by people and beliefs that you have trusted all of your life. I will be covering topics that are not main stream as well this information is out there for you to read and see with your own eyes all you have to do is look. If you're open to the truth the truth will present itself and set you free. All I want to do is present this information, not debate it.

"You will see it for yourself when you allow yourself to feel it so that you can believe it."

"You are in constant dialog with your creator you just thinking your not!!"

Point to it not teaching it, because all forms of truth are forms of truth, they are not (THE TRUTH). You cannot speak of the truth; it cannot be grasped in this place that I call EGO Land.

Think of me as a dog barking, I am repeating information that I have sifted thru over 20 yrs and have come to my own interpretation of my own experience.

This is not the truth, this is my truth at this moment and it will change as I unfold.

"EGO Land is set up as the ultimate program for limitation, to provide you the experience."

But one fundamental truth is I am not doing anything, you are not doing anything. You are being done. The awareness that perceives thru your body mind is using your biological meat suit as a vehicle to have an experience.

You think you are in the driver seat but you are only the passenger along for the ride and the name of the ride is EGO Land. Sometimes you take control of the wheel and the ride hits a couple of bumps in the road, sometimes it even crashes.

The best way to enjoy the ride is with your hands off the wheel and to be sitting in the passenger seat smiling.

"Stop judging and controlling your life, it's a game. You are awakening to your personal power and the nature of the illusion, your illusion."

4 stages of awakening to who you are and why you are here.

Stage one: you awake to the truth of who and what you are. Questioner Mode begins

Stage two: you become the apprentice and seek validation on the truth of whom and what you are. Questioner Mode still around but now you have added the Seeker Mode.

Stage three: you want to awaken others to the truth of whom and what they are. Teacher Mode kicks in you lose both the questioner and seeker. Now you are like a parrot you repeat the information you have collected in your own experience, seeking out others to validate the experience.

"True suffering is believing
the thoughts that arise are true.
You came to this world with NO
THING and you will leave with NO
THING."

Stage four: you stop all prior stages and know that no one needs to be fixed and no one is broken. You understand everyone is on the same path just different experiences. Only one experience having many experiences.

You allow life to move you instead you moving life. Mastery Mode. You now only observe instead of interfere or manipulate your experience. You now understand that talking is just talking, just like a dog barking.

So for me this began in 1998 and I ask the question why am I here and down the rabbit hole I went and the mis information and dis information rolled in.

"Memory never contains now!

Awareness is always expressing itself as the NOW moment."

Book after book, website after website and the questioner was born which gave birth to the seeker. Now my truth today is not my truth tomorrow so I have completed this book as a marker or a guide book for my children.

My first question is: Are we setup for failure from the beginning? Do we need the contrast and the struggle to operate within the GAME of Life? EGO Land.

What I am trying to say is all the content of our lives, its part of the story...the ride. The experience and we make our choice PRE BIRTH to experience certain things.

"Underneath every human being's cool rational exterior is a passion, you won't find the reason why he/she creates a style for himself unless you find the passion in them that drives them to need such a cover."

(Unknown Author)

So if you keep buying a lottery ticket thinking so bad you want to be a millionaire and you keep failing at it, maybe your not suppose to be a millionaire this time around.

Think of it like a roller coaster ride, before you get on each set of seats has a lane for you to file into. The ride may have up to 14 seats for 2 people per compartment. You choose who you like to come on your ride this time around. Example (your Family and Friends)

So you approach the ride you pick the lane that best suits the experience you like to have. Some pick the middle to just coast thru the ride the first time around. Others will pick the front as they have been on this ride many times and want the maximum result from the ride and others may pick the back as they have been on the front and middle and wish to continue the ride but are thinking of trying a different ride or perspective. Some people don't even get on the ride and sit on the side lines to see the reactions of other as they get on the ride and especially when they get off the ride.

"Everything is an illusion, past already happened, future isn't here and the only real time is NOW!" Meaning Right NOW!!

Even when the ride is over the ones that don't get on the ride will ask others how was it, what did you experience, should I try it.

So I would like to ask you in your life where do you see yourself on this roller coaster ride.

I call this place EGO land and it's the construct of a play ground for us to grow and unfold to reach our divine potential within the GAME. I shouldn't use the word reach because it's not something you obtain or get. It's something you remember and bring thru the character you are now playing.

"You would not have a deep driving desire or reoccurring fantasy to do something if you didn't have the capability to fulfill it."
(Unknown Author)

Are you playing the victim or addict and have manifested a disease in your life because you like attention or crying out for help.

Are you playing the good friend who is the shoulder to cry on and enjoys speaking about others and enjoy the drama and gossip?

Are you all the above or playing the role of many hats and can't keep up with all the TO Do's?

Are you playing the role of the seeker, teacher or the Guru? Jumping from material to technique to recruiting others to follow and experience your ride.

"Things don't change we change."

We have come from a place of purity and are still in a place of perfection, this hologram of our body, this meat suit we walk around in, is our vehicle to move within 3D space. We are multi dimension beings if you like it or not.

You may not be ready to hear this but you can ask yourselves if what you are reading is true. We are all hook up as a truth meter and I advise you before retaining any information to check in with your truth meter.

How does this information that I am giving you feel, not how does it fit in with your current belief structure but how does this feel to you.

"How much of your life is on automatic pilot?"

See we are losing our sense of feeling with the advancement of our modern technology. We are now hooked up not to feel but to be entertained at every moment. We have lost our connection to our divine spark; it's still there and never leaves. What this book will do is show you how strong is your signal? How much of your life is on automatic pilot?

I have come to the understand that things are not as they appear to be and we are not who we think we are.

That the limitations we but on ourselves are patterns of belief and habitual ways of moving within EGO land. We listen and absorb to much of others information or experience to see the comparison in our own daily experience.

"Are you making a living or living a life?"

When that comparison doesn't match up we think something is wrong and that we have to fix it to become better then the other person. We want to be happy and we strive for happiness in all our experiences. That is the program here in EGO Land and you can never get rid of the program its part of the game.

The game is how can you entertain me, what's in it for me. This place you are born into is a place to fulfill all your wants, needs and desires. It is set up like an amusement park or Circus with all its clowns, ring leaders, freak shows and scary rides and you are one of the characters in the park and you can choose what ride you like to be on. (FREE WILL)

You may be one of the people that hasn't been able to get on the roller coaster ride of life but have been on the side lines asking others about what's it like or you may like to sit and read about it.

"The game is how can you entertain me, what's in it for me."

I hope after you read this book you are ready to make one step and get on the ride even better jump to the front of the line and throw your hands up and let it all go. Just some words of advice about all the rides in EGO Land the more child like you are the more life will be able to move thru you to give you the ride of your life.

Some people are in EGO Land in a dream like daze, moving thru each experience (RIDE) to the next on auto pilot. They can't even see it's the same experience (RIDE) they have been on over and over again. Just the characters have changed and the scenery is different but the underlining experience is the same.

They are stuck in an experience loop, what is needed is to stop and step back out of the box to see how they keep repeating the same patterns.

"This place you are born into is a place to fulfill all your wants, needs and desires."

I am here to bring your attention to the patterns in your own experience to say stop, just for one second, one minute just stop and look around you. My remembering started when I asked a question to myself. Because what you learn from birth is information and the things you know really deep down know are true without someone teaching you and this comes thru in a feeling.

I call it the (AH Ha moment).

You Are Born Awake/Born Knowing!! Your Unborn Nature Never Sleeps. Only your body sleeps and your being is awake and playing in every experience if you're aware of it or not. (Out of Body Experiences)

Life is not a puzzle to be solved but a game that wants to be played. This is an invitation to stop what ever search you are on because deep down at the fundamental core it's a search for happiness. Wholeness of what you already are, it's not a process it's a knowing, a remembering.

"Where is everything when you're not thinking about it?"

Knowing that you know, and isn't it time for you to stop the chase and take a look around, we all carry this wound of separation from the whole. We try everything to fill it up and become whole again only to feel stuck or lost.

If you have been drawn to open this book you are ready to rest and allow yourself to give up. Give in to yourself, rest with your being and be satisfied with what is here.

You are the teacher and the student; you are your own healer and guru. What happens when you stop, just being still in silence.

"Life is not a puzzle to be solved but a game that wants to be played."

Imagine this nothing happening, no concepts, ideas or beliefs, just emptiness. In a split second in your life, how ever you are evaluating your experience. Stop

Let go of the ultimate prize of spiritual enlightenment because I have a secret you are already that. So take a deep breath and exhale. Fall deeply in love with what you have and who you are. In this state of gratitude you are free to flow with life.

If you are still reading this you have exhausted the seeker in you. You are ready to meet the true you. You are ready to let go of your story.

"Let go of the ultimate prize of spiritual enlightenment because I have a secret you are already that."

I cannot give you a technique on how to do this just point you to it. I cannot tell you the truth of who you are because your mind with grasp for it or push it away.

To really understand what I am speaking about is something you cannot grasp with your mind but only with your being. That little spark in you that never ages and never dies.

You think you are doing it but you are not, you are being done. This book is not a teaching it's a pointer. We are all on a path, a road, a quest and that road leads us and pulls us.

"Your EGO is a closed loop. Its job is to keep you entertained and the program of EGO Land is a surrender program, so let go"

It's an energetic pull of our own energy back to the source of all to remember who we are.

EGO land is showing you the limitlessness of limitation and separation.

You are here to have an experience, you have arrived!! You are here SO PLAY!! Get on the ride and scream.

"You are timeless awareness travelling thru the world of the mind to be a person in time. You're unlimited and you are wanting an experience of limitation."

You are this divine spark in human form.... Surprise, get used to it!! Accept it, and Believe it, Understand every moment, every person you encounter is an aspect of you, it is you. If your belief system cannot grasp this idea, then you need to return this book for a full refund.

I am writing this for you as you but I am me speaking to you to help you remember who you are. You are in EGO Land in order to experience the duality of what is to be separate from your self. Your 5 senses will only allow so much of what is around you thru. This is the beginning of the illusion.

The difference between you and me is I know I am writing this to myself to wake you up to yourself.

"The difference between you and me is I know I am writing this to myself to wake you up to yourself."

Everything in EGO land is set up as a surrender program, the more you let go of who you think you are the more will unfold of who you really are.

EGO land is a place for you to experience Anger/Hurt/Fear and return to Love.

You come here to EGO Land over and over again, lifetime after lifetime. Playing this character, after character to move thru all experiences that have anger, hurt, and fear at the route of the experience.

"You are the creation of yourself.
You create everything you want,
need or desire."

The underlining experience is love that encompasses them all. If you peel back the layers, you will have arrived, you are now in touch with your divine spark.

To be here is to enter a beautiful, shared illusion that gives you complete power over what you can create for your own personal reality; this is how powerful you are. Within EGO Land we believe that we are looking at a separate person, you are not, we are ONE. One experience playing the part of many.

You are the creation of yourself. You create everything you want, need or desire. You have chosen this life. You have chosen the obstacles and experience before you came into this life. What you can be are your self-beliefs about what you think you can or cannot do.

"This is a playground of experiences; reality is a mirror of you teaching you to not take yourself so seriously."

This is a playground of experiences; reality is a mirror of you teaching you to not take yourself so seriously. You are exploring yourself in a space-time mirror. So what you choose to believe is what you create to be your reality. You change your reality by changing your beliefs about it and yourself.

Your perception is an act of creation. You choose what you want to see or experience for yourself with your entire reality. You draw everything to you like a magnet, good or bad.

Once awakening happens you will move thru 4 stages to remember your own personal power to lead your experience of reality to become more fluid and direct. This is to enter lucid living with your divine spark where what you desire is quickly manifest. The key to lucid living is the allowance of change; the manifesting of the unknown into the known.

"Allowance is acceptance. To change your reality you have to first accept it."

Allowance is acceptance. To change your reality you have to first accept it. When you reject your reality you are in denial of your personal power, leaving you feeling blocked.

None acceptance is holding on to something with both hands so if your hands are full how you do expect anything if you can't have your hands open. If both your hands are full they cannot receive anything, so drop the old patterns and receive all your want, needs and desires.

To understand and accept that you are creating your reality, release attachment to any thought of how your life should be and instead love what is. Accept and be in the NOW.

"You need to stop grasping at the future and pushing away the past."

You need to stop grasping at the future and pushing away the past.

You need to take complete responsibility for every element of your reality.

This is to love your choice. It is to love yourself. You are the creation of yourself.

Release your fear. Stand in your fear because your power stops where your fear begins. Under anger is hurt, under hurt is fear and under fear is love. You are love.

"Release your fear. Stand in your fear because your power stops where your fear begins"

Fear is fear of the unknown, fear of your unlimited power. Fear creates limitation. EGO Land is set up as the ultimate program for limitation, to provide you the experience. There is a natural, beautiful flow to life that can only arise when you let go of the control that arises through fear.

Let go and let your spirit come thru. You are remembering who you are and forgetting the story of who you think you are.

Stop judging and controlling your life, it's a game. The game is to have fun and find JOY in everything you do. When you do this you release struggle and enter effortless creation.

"Under anger is hurt, under hurt is fear and under fear is love. You are love returning to itself"

Nothing should be hard, your divine spark moves with ease. Everything is simple and perfect, so love what is not what you think it should be. You are awakening to your personal power and the nature of the illusion, your illusion.

This is a natural process and requires no effort. This means opening and following your heart. To look outside of your self is to deny your own power but when you look inside is to awaken to your true purpose.

This is your freedom: believe whatever your heart feels to believe. This is to live in the Now.

"You are not broken and you don't need to be fixed. You just need to remember who you truly are."

Awaken to the awesome power of all your spirit and release judgment of both yourself and the world. You are not broken and you don't need to be fixed. You just need to remember who you truly are.

What if I could point you to a place that you have been seeking and searching for your entire life?

This is a space of peace, love, joy and laughter. You are always in this space that you are familiar with but lost somewhere down the line of your experience.

"We are all seeking, searching, looking for a piece to complete this puzzle we call our life our being. "

We are all seeking, searching, looking for a piece to complete this puzzle we call our life our being.

We look for meaning and reason in the things we do or the experiences we have or create.

We so often look outside of ourselves for the truth of our being. We long for the closeness and oneness of our creator our source.

We jump from class to class, teacher to teacher, book to book.

"The primary illusion is that you seek, question and think something is wrong. That is what has you chasing your tail."

The primary illusion is that you seek, question and think something is wrong. That is what has you chasing your tail.

You are in a loop of experiences. Until you exhaust what is fueling your quest/mission you will never be free.

Let go of reason and meaning, let go of your craving and thirsts for more of what you're addicted to, what entertains you is what is blocking you.

Let go of the desire to win in every situation, to be entertained by someone or something and bring something to the table instead of taking something off the table.

"You are in a loop of experiences, over and over again the wheel of life goes round"

Your mind will always want more and must have more of anything you desire, allow your desire to burn out.

Stop running from not being satisfied and you're grasping at wholeness. Every thought you have is untrue, nothing that comes out of your mind is the truth. It is only an explanation created from your belief structure.

Suffering is believing the thoughts that arise are true, your body will duplicate the thought to give you the feeling of what you seek, and we all grasp for pleasure and run from pain. To truly see what you're seeking you need to drop all your beliefs and accept what is.

"Let go of reason and meaning, let go of your craving and thirsts for more of what you're addicted to, what entertains you is what is blocking you. "

What is here right now without all the bells and whistles? All the ideas, concepts and beliefs, what is present right now.

Close your eyes and go within, see that you will never stop your mind from thinking; you can only turn it down. Bring down the volume. When you do this you allow space, a gap to open up because nothing is present, when you go within.

NO-THING, but pure awareness. Out of nothing becomes something. Every thought that includes (Spiritual materialism) is a projection of a concept and belief pattern. Pure awareness is not spiritual its emptiness laughing.

"Let go of the desire to win in every situation, to be entertained by someone or something and bring something to the table instead of taking something off the table."

There is nothing wrong with all your concepts, ideas and beliefs but to have any attachment to them you are bound and not free.

I say have all your concepts, ideas and beliefs fulfilled to the end.

Exhaust them all until they all burn out and fade away. That is why you are to have an experience.

You came to this world with NO THING and you will leave with NO THING.

If you think you are what you have (stuff), You think you are what you do (JOB), You think you are what people think of you (Reputation), You think you are separate from everyone and your creator, you are the creator.

"There is nothing wrong with all your concepts, ideas and beliefs but to have any attachment to them you are bound to them and you are not free."

Your natural state without all the bells and whistles is always giving, providing and not expecting anything in return. To open this GAP and see what arises start to act like what you are seeking.

In order to get in touch with NO THING you must do nothing and drop everything to have nothing. To see the divine spark, (your spark) it will cost you only one thing, everything you believe in.

All of your want needs and desires, all your cravings and thrusts, all your concepts, ideas and beliefs have to fall away and allow yourself to come thru.

"In order to get in touch with NO THING you must do nothing and drop everything to have nothing."

Think of all your concepts, ideas and beliefs as a shield, this shield is fear; it's an attachment to an idea of how we want the experience to enfold.

Nothing is right wrong good or bad it just is. All of your want needs and desires, all your cravings and thrusts all that entertains you is what blocks you and keeps you in an experience loop until you have exhausted the energy that you have invested in it.

So when you have an experience have no attachment to it or project the outcome in your mind. Stop grasping for experiences and pushing them away, just allow them to unfold without any manipulation or expectations.

"Nothing is right wrong good or bad
it just is!"

Don't think of it as something that is good or bad, right or wrong. See most people are dragged around thru their experience like a dog on a leash with all their ideas which is mind or feelings which is their emotion about the experience they are having.

See when you start to awaken to your true nature everything becomes neutral the first stop is on the level of mind and it will grasp on to anything you can't let go of and even if you say your going to let go of everything but we all keep one or two thoughts usually we keep the good ones, the ones that comfort us like the thought of {I am}.

See thought comes from emptiness....nothing so when it comes out of nothing and becomes something then right at that moment it's UNTRUE. Even the good thoughts of what you think about any experience.

"The problem isn't getting into the NOW. We need to look at all the ways we bring ourselves out of the NOW moment."

You are perfectly whole already and awakening to the truth of what you are is very plain, with no name, no label, no flavor, no sense, no texture, no big bang, and no grandiose entrance. It's always been here allowing all experiences to unfold with no judgment, no idea of what is right wrong good or bad, just experiencing everything as it is.

If you like to meet this part of you, you don't even have to ask and you don't even have to do anything. Don't think of a thought, a technique, a process or a way to manipulate the experience of what has been always here and is everywhere and everything.

Give yourself permission to stop, stop the search, stop the control, stop the manipulation, and stop the interference of the natural flow of life. As life is living you, you are not living it. You don't have Awareness, Awareness has you.

"You don't have Awareness,
Awareness has you. "

The construct of reality is Awareness and the content is you. You don't need to look for it or grasp for it or push it away because you can't get away from it. You think you can and that is the Primary Illusion.

So now I know I am this divine spark......now what?

To understand that you are timeless awareness choosing to be a person in time is not enough. You have to feel it, embody it. Most of us are all tech'd out. I see more and more people walking down the road, with ear plugs, sunglasses on, cell phone texting, listing to MP3 player and talking to someone at the same time thru an ear piece.

"The construct of reality is
Awareness and the content is you."

We are not in our bodies we are being pulled out of the NOW present moment of future plans or reliving past experiences. Be aware of when you are pulled out of presence that includes everything that pulls your attention way from the NOW moment.

The key, the doorway, the opening to understand this is thru the space of allowing EGO and Being to coexist. Those spaces where you're not taking yourself seriously, its that play state of your being.

The space between the 2 worlds when you inhale or exhale, when your not grasping and not pushing away.

"The worst EGO of them all is a Spiritual EGO."

The worst EGO of them all is a Spiritual EGO. The Spiritual Trap is so slippery and sticky it can take lifetimes to come out of this experience loop.

The reason is you believe your collective thoughts and experiences about how you think things are from second hand information and have ritualistic experiences to confirm how some else or divine being was or acted like.

So you try to obtain what that one persons experience for your self or mimic thru practice (auto pilot) the ways they did or have written down in a divine text on how you should perform and repeat over and over again to obtain the same experience.

"You cannot be someone else, you can only be you. "

When you are here in this lifetime to have your own experiences not someone else's. You cannot be someone else, you can only be you.

There will never be another you ever. This combination of MIND/BODY/SPIRIT will never exist in this order ever again.

You must live each day like you are dying. Your body is regenerating every minute of the day, the body you have now is not the same body you had as a teenager but the divine spark you came in with is the same as you where then and now.

"Let go of giving things meaning and reason. Accept what is and let go of how you think it should be. "

So to feel it you need to release all purpose of being of who you think you are and allow what is to come thru. Drop your story, let it go. There is no mission, if you want a mission, a purpose then your mission is to be present, authentic and respond in the moment.

To do this is to live lucidly and simple just be in the moment, be aware of the moment right NOW.

Get out of the mind of past or future and be present in what is happening. Let go of giving things meaning and reason. Accept what is and let go of how you think it should be.

This is not a teaching; this is a way of being. Like I said at the beginning all I am is a pointer to the truth of who and what you are.

"The EGO (mind) is a closed loop its job is to keep you entertained"

I can't give you what you are. It's an experience that is so plain you miss it ever time you wake up and start your day. It's already here and we look out there for it.

Enjoy this moment its all you have....your ego brings you into the past and future and tells you stories of that might happen.

It gives you things to do, give you things to fix and figure out. What I am suggesting is to let go and rest into your being.

The EGO(mind) is a closed loop that will have you chasing your tail until you exhaust the seeker.

When you STOP searching for what you think you are and rest in what you are, the truth can be revealed.

"Your being doesn't think it just is. Stop doing and start being. "

If you understand that there is no such thing as a true thought you will be free to enjoy your own energy.

The mind is a tool that creates thoughts. In EGO Land you need your mind to operate within the GAME it comes with the meat suit.

All thoughts are not true, every thought you have is either an excuse or a strategy to get something to hold on to or push something away.

All of this is manipulation of not seeing your true self.

Your being doesn't think it just is. Stop doing and start being.

"You will never get rid of your EGO; you can only turn the volume down."

You will never get rid of your EGO; you can only turn the volume down. You can have all your techniques, concepts, philosophies, religions, and ideas all you want just don't believe in them.

They are stories, just like stories in a book at bedtime.

When you believe in them you're lost in the world of the mind. We live in the world of the mind right now.

All of what you see is possible because of the tool of the mind.

I am here to pass on my experience in order to allow others to awaken/remember who they truly are. I found once I let go of what I thought should happen and allowed what is, all my energy centers blew open.

"Instead of taking something from every experience you, start to bring something to every experience."

When you stopped resistance and creating the story of (ME) that includes the spiritual story of me, you start to open up and stand in your own energy instead of the energy of past or future of the MIND.

You choose not to be entertained and your EGO has a hard time because it feeds off resistance to everything. Its job is to entertain you, DISTRACT you.

When you begin this shift, this awareness of your unborn self watching the experience you are now free to make different choices. Instead of living in your usual habitual way of living, you start to feel fluid, lucid and free.

"You are spirit moving thru the world of the mind having a human experience within time."

Instead of taking something from every experience you, start to bring something to every experience. You start give because you know giving is to receive.

You will start to see the divine encounter that you are having with everyone around you. That you are meeting yourself, speaking with yourself, that a mirror is being shown to you in every experience you have.

If you want to remember faster of who you are simply stop everything and that means everything, look at the things you are resisting and stand in your FEAR.

LIFE IS LIVING THRU YOU!!

Your fear is the doorway; thru fear is the open gate to what you have been looking for.

You're POWER STOPS where your FEAR begins. You are not a person seeking for a spiritual awakening (enlightment) you are already enlightened.

You are spirit moving thru the world of the mind having a human experience within time.

This will not go away; you will have glimpses of energetic openings and Aha moments. Enjoy them in the moment and set them down.

Do not grasp at them or try to recreate them or take them with you.

"Remember when someone is in pain they give pain and vice versa."

There is nothing you must do except is to be awake in the moment, and everything else takes care of itself. It takes trust and surrender to live this way, letting life unfolds for you rather than directing it yourself with the mind.

Realize that you are eternal awareness that never changes, and it doesn't need to be fixed or healed, it doesn't have to evolve. The real you is already whole... it's not a process.

LIFE IS LIVING THRU YOU!!

Remember when someone is in pain they give pain and vice versa.

Nothing is Right/Wrong....Good or Bad it just IS.

"You can have all your want, needs and desires meet, just don't have any attachment to them."

Let go of doing and rest into being. Let go of a belief in something and you will be free.

You are free you are safe so take a rest and see what is present. Welcome what is here with no denial, everything is included.

Everything I mean everything, all the good and all the bad, all the right and all the wrong.

Accept what is and it will show you where you are, you are here now and all is well just stop looking for it because everything you need is here.

So everything that you grasp for or push away such as a teacher, Guru, special technique, book, CD, class or manipulation that you come up with in your own mind, is in fact a reason your not satisfied with your present experience.

"You are having an experience, enjoy your experience. Let go of your story line. The most important moment of your life happens—when you stop reacting to the button being pushed and start living!"

So this includes every want need or desire is to pull you out of the present moment. You can have all your want, needs and desires meet, just don't have any attachment to them. Don't believe in them.

When you have a want, need or desire and you place your vision on the outcome, on how you want it to unfold on how you want it to happen, you have taken your being out of the equation.

You are living on a planet that was created by a force of energy, you are apart of that energy so you are a creator as well. When you force a creation you force out the creator part out of you and now you're left with the tool (Mind/ EGO).

"You are not doing anything you are being done."

All you must do is relax, stop and feel your being come thru. No pushing or grasping, No remembering or imagining.

If I told you there is no mission!! What button on you will be pushed and you will return this book or burn it. We all walk around with some kind of button, some more then others. Some big and some small.

We are all walking around with these hair triggers pointing them, waiting to have them pulled so we can express ourselves. How many buttons are you walking around with?

Each lifetime you either accumulate more or less and the mission if you like to call it a mission is to recognize and let go of them. The mission is to be human, to have an experience in EGO Land.

We all suffer from separation, all of us meaning everyone has this wired into them. Stop running from it, seeking and searching for who you think you are and be who you are.

You are having an experience, enjoy your experience. Let go of your story line. The most important moment of your life happens—when you stop reacting to the button being pushed and start living! It's the choice you make to move toward a life in flow instead of a life in EGO.

"Formless into form and form into formless this is the nature of reality."

It's the moment you start living a life of meaning and begin playing instead of working! Are you ready to know the way? Isn't time someone gave you the rule book, of no rules. No excuses!! What is your excuse?

All excuses are shields around your button that you may not want to be pushed. I say push them all, set them all off, have a weekend where all you do is push these buttons.

Get them out of the way and move on with your life.

Your ego/mind is tricking you, so correct your mind, and think soft. Be flexible, be open, be able to move, allow yourself to be moved.

"To see the divine spark, in everything it costs one thing everything you believe."

Allow your button to be pushed, stand in your fear when the button goes off. Because the biggest energetic layer around you is anger, after that the layer is smaller around hurt and the thinnest layer is fear. So small you can't even see until you push a button then you are so sensitive to it you can feel it.

When you feel something you don't want to experience it but the truth is you have to move thru fear to get to love.

This is the OPENING and most of this layer around everyone one is around our hearts.

So now what, what is next, well what to do, how to do, when to do....we all like to do and really you don't have to do anything but some people need a helping hand.

"The divine spark in our minds IS NOT A BEING or a force up in the sky with a big white beard. It is you, it is nothing becoming something."

If you want to do something, first thing get straight what you really are, because otherwise you're EGO self will be doing all your inquiring.

Fear feeds on denial, if you're stuck in a religious belief just understand all religion is just another costume party.

I know that pushed some buttons, can't wait for the emails on that one, but the core of ego is a gigantic NO!

True power is connecting with your divine spark -- it's not a personal power and true compassion isn't something you feel for another person. It is when you know in every fiber of my being that this person in front of me..... Is me. I am looking at me.

"Stop your thrust for wanting. Let yourself be satisfied with what is here now."

To see the divine spark, it costs one thing -- everything you believe.

The divine spark in our minds IS NOT A BEING or force up in the sky with a big white beard. It is you, it is nothing becoming something.

Stop your thrust for wanting. Let yourself be satisfied with what is here now.

We have all the techniques on how to get into the NOW moment, that isn't the problem. We need to look at all the ways we bring ourselves out of the NOW moment.

"Nobody has the power to make you miserable it's an inside job."

Nobody has the power to make you miserable it's an inside job, there's always a hidden belief when you react to being squeezed or pressured, when your button goes off.

Even if our agenda is 'good,' we are transmitting an agenda with its little bit of division, even this book. We are operating in EGO Land you need division for the program to run.

So any teaching from A to Zen, they all serve their purpose in moving you to the next step.

There is no secret book in the sky that has your life's purpose written in it. You don't need to go thru life looking for what you already know. You choose the life you live and you do this with your thoughts if you like it or not. You attracted everything into your life.

"There is no secret book in the sky that has your life's purpose written in it. You don't need to go thru life looking for what you already know."

What Buttons do you have on?

From low to high, the levels of consciousness are: shame, guilt, apathy, grief, fear, desire, anger, pride, courage, neutrality, willingness, acceptance, reason, love, joy, peace.

An increase from one level to another will result in enormous change in your life.

Shame - Just a step above death. You're probably contemplating suicide at this level. Think of this as self-directed hatred. I don't want to be here.

Guilt - A step above shame, but you still may be having thoughts of suicide. You think of yourself as an unworthy, unable to forgive yourself for past experiences.

Apathy - Feeling hopeless or victimized. The state of learned helplessness. Many homeless people are stuck here. Blaming others.

Grief - A state of perpetual sadness and loss. You might drop down here after losing a loved one. Remembering the past, holding on to the past.

Fear - Seeing the world as dangerous and unsafe. Us against them, you are different from me so I keep you at a distance. I don't understand.

Desire - Is feeding addiction, craving, and thrust — for money, approval, power, fame, etc. Spiritualism, Consumerism, Materialism. Smoking/drinking/drugs and sexual exploration. Feeding every want need and thrust for something more.

Example: becoming Spiritual is another form of an addiction just labeled something different.

It's the Spiritual EGO tricking you.

Anger - Is frustration, often from not having your desires met at any level. You blame others and are not accepting what is, you are projecting how you think it should be, instead of allowing.

Pride – You finally start to feel good, but it's a false feeling. It's dependent on external circumstances (money, prestige, etc), you identify with what you have your stuff. It's all about me; me, me and what can you do for me. How can you entertain me and my pride? You become so closely enmeshed in your beliefs that you see an attack on your beliefs as an attack on you.

Courage – You now begin to have an understanding of and interest in personal growth; You start to see your future as an improvement upon your past, rather than a continuation of the same. You let go of the past but now your are grasping for the future. Very tricky place to be with your EGO who wants you in the future and loves you in the past.

Neutrality – This level is epitomized by the phrase, "live and let live." It's flexible, relaxed, and unattached. Whatever happens, you roll with the punches. You don't have anything to prove. A very comfortable place but slippery slop and very sticky for the EGO to use and hold you into a pattern of beliefs. The level of complacency and laziness. You're taking care of your needs, but you don't push yourself too hard.

Willingness - Now that you're basically safe and comfortable, you start using your energy more effectively. Just getting by isn't good enough anymore. You begin caring about doing a good job.

Acceptance - Now a powerful shift happens, and you awaken to the possibilities of living proactively. At the level of willingness you've become competent, and now you want to put your abilities to good use. This is the level of setting and achieving goals. You're off the coach and out in the world.

Reason - At this level you transcend the emotional aspects of the lower levels and begin to think clearly and rationally. This is the level of healing. The way I see it, when you reach this level, you become capable of using your reasoning abilities to their fullest extent. You've reached the point where you say, "Wow. I can do all this stuff, and I know I must put it to good use.

Love - It's unconditional love, a permanent understanding of your connectedness with all that exists. You have a know you are Awareness interacting with itself. You are no longer living in service to your EGO. Your intuition becomes extremely strong. You react out of love and a knowing it is what it is.

Joy - this state is the NOW. There's no more need to set goals and make detailed plans — the expansion of your consciousness allows you to operate at a much higher level. A near-death experience can temporarily bump you to this level. You realize nothing needs to be done it all has its place.

Peace - Total transcendence. Unshakable awareness of what is.

"The idea of meditation is not to become a good mediator but to be aware of the manipulation you are doing without consciously being aware of it."

So when I say do nothing I don't mean sit on the coach and eat chips and watch TV all day.

Any tool you get or come across your path is a tool. Like a crow bar will pry open a crack in order to let something get in? In this case you are cracking the shell around you to let something out.

Use these tools and please put them down, do not get attached to them. I strongly recommend burning this book after you read it, or throwing it out.

I am only a pointer and this truth for me will change so for now it is written down but don't take it and chew on it for to long. Don't even pass it on to a friend. My purpose isn't to fix anyone or to awaken anyone but to respond with love and to embody love.

"Asking for something is prayer and meditation is listening for the answer."

To be flexible with my thinking enough to be moved in the direction of the greater good.

For example the idea of meditation is not to become a good mediator but to be aware of the manipulation you are doing without consciously being aware of it. We get lost in the world of the mind so easily because you are in the world of the mind. (EGO Land).

Couple of tools I find work for me.

- Meditation

- Prayer

- Visualization

- Gratitude

- Detachment

"All that you thrust for and feed on is blocking you and dragging you around in an experience loop. "

Asking for something is prayer and meditation is listening for the answer. We think in pictures so visualization is the creation of what experience you like to have. Gratitude is the expression of being thankful for what you already have and detachment is allowing for anything to enfold. Right/Wrong Good/Bad.

When you see your truth it's a big thing what you are trying to uncover in your self inquiry, in order to peel back the first layer you must stop all outside influences and attachments you have to EGO Land. All that you thrust for and feed on is blocking you and dragging you around in an experience loop.

To peel this first layer away you must first accept it and know you alone have built this prison in your own experience. If you cannot do this, then stop now and return this book until you are ready to be set free. This first step is crucial because it keeps you locked in and engaged in habitual patterns that will not serve your highest good.

"Listening to me is like a dog barking, I am only pointing to the truth"

To many of us get entrapped in the idea of being spiritual and it's a nice idea but it has nothing to do with your true being. If I personally wanted to be around a bunch of EGO's 24/7, I would like them all to be spiritual because it makes it more bearable.

We all need to take personal responsibility for our own truth. We shop around from teacher to Guru looking for that next big spiritual experience or energetic opening or final destination.

There is no prize at the end of the game, no medal or trophy. You are not here in EGO Land to gain anything but to come to the realization that you have to loose everything.

"To many of us get entrapped in the idea of being spiritual and it's a nice idea but it has nothing to do with your true being."

No secret teaching, secret text or holy book will give you the map to what you're looking for; it can only light the way for a little while and it will only be a tool to get you part of the way.

The rest of the way is walked on your own in the moment in the none seeking moment, it is not something you can carry with you, hold on to or accumulate on your way.

The space between the gaps in your thoughts is the place I am pointing to.

"Your true being isn't spiritual it just is"

When that gap is there, the awareness leaps out of the unknown into the known. The crow bar (meditation) is needed to pull open that gap just enough to allow a spark to come thru.

Timeless comes thru time (Ego Land) and plays with its separation dualistic nature of being. Realization of this truth does not liberate you from Ego Land it only lights your way.

Shining light on the path of where you are so that you can see your way home. How ever you are evaluating your experience stop and look at what is right in front of you.

"Are you ready to lose your story, drop your character?"

Every experience is an experience with yourself and is a sacred gift to yourself as a choice point for you to choose for the return home.

You must be willing to stand alone—in the unknown, with no reference to the known or the past or any conditioning. This is the way thru fear and this is the path of love.

In truth the entire spiritual endeavor is a very simple thing: so for some it may be very easy, while for others it may be more difficult.

"You must be willing to stand alone—in the unknown, with no reference to the known or the past or any conditioning."

Are you ready to lose your story, drop your character? Because you can be in the world but not be moved by the world, even when you get glimpses of your true nature you will still come back to your old story.

So what this means is that you start to wake up from the character you are playing within EGO Land. You start to see how you are influenced and who pushes your buttons.

You start to see what drags you around and what habitual habits you have been slaved to. You start to catch yourself in the act of being an EGO in EGO Land.

"The awareness that perceives thru your body mind is using your biological meat suit as a vehicle to have an experience. "

You are now IN THE LIGHT, in the know of the patterns and cycles that keep you locked in the ways that are not serving you or your greatest potential.

This doesn't mean you lose the character; you are still who you are just now you are aware of the parts you have been playing. You are now aware of the whole story instead of just the one character role.

You still have to go to work, feed the kids and play with your friends.

"You allow life to move you instead you moving life."

Just something is different; you now feel it's not about ME it's about US.

The ME has now SHIFTED to WE.

Realization to the true awareness of what you are is a deep realization of what you are as an experience. What is it that is feeling? What is it that is thinking or sensing? This is not about coming up with the right name for it, so don't name it for a moment. It's about just noticing, just experiencing. Feel it. Sense it.

So when your mind pulls you catch it in the act and be aware of it the next time and the next time it comes around. It will not go away, it cannot because its part of your meat suit for you to play in EGO Land.

"Just something is different; you now feel it's not about ME it's about US.

The ME has now SHIFTED to WE."

So whatever you're vice is, what ever entertains you, it can be drinking, drugs, sex or spiritually to name a few of the many. Find out what is the pattern in your life. The cycle that needs to be broken, the repetitive experience loop you find yourself in.

If you don't deal with it this time around it will come around again don't worry it always does. In a different set of circumstances with different characters to play different roles but rest assure the underlining principals will be present to help you in your choice point.

Once you recognize the choice point you shift the energy, you tip the balance. Everything is in balance, if you start to steal, manipulate, cheat and take advantage of another you might get away with it now and you may have a ticket to ride for this life time but the next it will balance out.

"This meat suit we walk around in is our vehicle to move within 3D space. We are multi dimension beings if you like it or not."

Every experience will set off a change reaction from the smallest cycle to the largest experience. So something from 20 past lifetimes ago will intersect with this life time's larger choice at a certain cycle where the elements for a specific life experience for you to have a choice point to change your path to the return home will occur.

Some times it will feel overwhelming and uncontrollable, like the world is out to get you. That is the gift, that is the grace that is the divine encounter for you to recognize that as the ultimate gift to yourself.

To see beyond the EGO Land program and reach for more then what's in this for me, what can I get out of this situation, how can I be entertained. You now can bring something to the experience instead of taking away from the experience.

"EGO land is showing you the limitlessness of limitation and separation."

You can now shift into the new and let go of the old experience loop that you have been stuck in. If you cannot see the pattern, if you cannot see the loop of experience and the character changes, it can be because you are fearful of the out come.

In order to see any pattern or experience loop for what it is you have to see what you are resistant to.

All resistance is the energy signature of the experience loop. Where you find any resistance to a situation, or an experience you would rather avoid that is your open gate.

"In order to see any pattern or experience loop for what it is you have to see what you are resistant to."

That is the entry point to the beginning of your enfoldment into a new paradigm; it's a new way of looking at your world, your experience, and a broader perception.

To allow this is to stand in it and face any resistance or fear. Stand in the middle of the resistance, experience the whole situation for what it brings and holds for you. Everyone is different and moving thru different experiences but there is only one experience happening.

To stand in it is to move thru it and on the other side of this experience, the loop will be broken. Now this is not to say another experience isn't waiting to be manifested because surprise there is.

"In EGO Land we believe that we are looking at a separate person, you are not, we are ONE. One experience playing the part of many."

But it will not be the same reoccurring experience with different characters. You are now free to play instead of reliving old patterns and old content.

This can carry on into many life times; you can get it now or not. You don't have to do anything but have chosen to be here now.

So be here now and being here now means to respond to your experience now. The problem isn't how to be here now it's to see how many things bring you away from here and now.

See we all want to be more, get more, have more and enjoy more. This drive for more is hard wired inside each and every one of us; this is the drive for happiness the striving but never arriving because it is endless. It is limitless; you are limitless so you will never stop this drive.

"The problem isn't how to be here now it's to see how many things bring you away from here and now."

You are continuously unfolding to become something and once that something has been achieved another something is in line. There is no end goal, no end game, no prize or trophy but to be what is.

So to be flexible enough in your thoughts, aware enough in your perception and relaxed enough with your EGO to allow you enough space to PLAY.

The more child like you are the less you take your experience seriously the easier your experience will be.

Your EGO mind wants it to be serious, needs it to be figured out. Its job is to try and maintain order within chaos, but it's clumsy and noisy. It produces noisy thoughts, feelings, beliefs, or opinions.

"The more child like you are the less you take your experience seriously the easier your experience will be."

It needs to search for the right concept and idea in order to justify actions. It's always moving and looking for the right thing to happen and once you move your focus away from it you start to notice something else is present.

Something that is not as noisy or trying to manipulate the experience with an old past experience or a future hope on how the new experience should unfold.

When we look too teachers and teachings for this spark of our divine nature it seems that we can only touch the surface and only get a taste or first kiss.

When we have the experience we start to look for more of what we think we are missing and get caught in a loop of seeking to explain what has happened or how can I replicate that same experience again. Just like a drug user searching for his first high that can never be reached because the first kiss is always the best one.

"You change your reality by changing your beliefs about it and yourself. "

So as we move thru our experience we tend to belief the character of the external being because so much is validating our experience in our daily life.

We have our friends, family and co-workers showing us that we are doing something right or we are doing something wrong.

We try to be always in the right but nothing is right wrong good or bad it just is think of it as neutral, plain, blank, or simply emptiness laughing.

"You need to take complete responsibility for every element of your reality. "

So if it feels like and looks like all this is repetitive talk, you are correct it's exactly that, just like a dog barking.

There is no truth within this book only arrow's pointing to the truth and you may have some resonance with the transmission of the truth.

And yes this is a nice concept and I could be wrong but that is why you have to have your own experience to find out for yourself what am I pointing too because you will never be at peace if you are caught up in the character you are playing in EGO LAND.

Why are you here? You are here to have an experience and to play.

What is this life for? You need this environment to have the comparison of the opposite of your true nature.

What is my life's purpose? You are to be present in the now moment and flexible in your thoughts to response to every experience with unconditional love to allow your unborn nature to be expressed thru your born nature.

Who are you? You are timeless awareness choosing to be a person in time to have an experience thru the mind.

You Are Emptiness Laughing!!

Send me your thoughts by email:
urgodgetoverit@yahoo.ca

www.emptinesslaughing.com

Biography

Born the older of 2 boys from my father's first marriage, then my parents separated when I was 3yrs old and we went to live with my mother.

I was born Catholic and went to a Catholic school until I was 6 yrs old when my mother became a Pentecostal Christian. I was entrenched in the Pentecostal religion 24/7 up until I was 13yrs old when I went to live with my father.

I went thru high school more as an observer and found myself in college doing the same thing. I wasn't one to follow but still had a normal childhood.

I would go visit my mother for a week at a time at my grandmother's house with my aunt.

We would all sit around the dinner table and they would argue about religion. My grandmother was a devoted Catholic, my mother a Pentecostal Pastor/Missionary and my aunt a Jehovah's Witness.

Now I would sit back and listen and rapid fire questions to them all of which they could not answer.

One I would always ask is "Why is there an old man in the sky who creates a place called (HELL) if he loves you so much." And "Why does this GOD need money all the time if he is so powerful?" and "Why do we need to go thru someone else to get to know him direct?" oh and one last thing in the sacred text written thousands of years ago why is there is no mention of Dinosaurs?

I was 13yrs and they couldn't give me a straight answer and all the answers were based on a word called (FAITH).

For me faith is built upon belief and belief is built upon evidence. Evidence is the feeling in any experience.

This is why I always check in with my truth meter when I read any source of information outside of myself before I take it on as belief.

I strongly suggest you do the same even with this book.

I really don't have any beliefs, I have concepts and ideas but I don't believe in them.

So as a young boy I was in the middle of a religious war zone with my family at both ends. Actually it wasn't that bad they were very nice to each other but it gave me a great starting point.

So for me in my teen years I had a good foundation once I start to explore drinking, girls (sex) and drugs. I was able to make some good decisions.

I started out working in the restaurant industry and worked my way up to bartender. I stayed in the industry for 20 yrs, with my last job being in a major downtown club.

Now the lifestyle of a bartender is what I compare to living like a Rock Star. You sleep all day, work 2 days out of the week; make the same money or more as a full time job. You have access to Sex/ Drugs and Alcohol 24/7. This experience loop is very hard to break.

That part of my life I saw how low you can go on auto pilot (experience Loop), I had so many good friends die from drinking/driving and from overdosing on drugs to becoming alcoholics.

I was a part of that world but I was fortunate to have a good foundation to be in it but not devoured by it.

Having seen what people can do to themselves weekend after weekend I was able to make the comparison on what do I want for myself.

I had a choice point too continue in that same experience loop or to break the connection.

I choose to break that connection and once that connection was severed an energetic opening happened. You see it takes a lot of energy to keep the EGO personality in place. Once you let it go you give room for a different energy to grow within your experience.

You will never get rid of your EGO, it isn't a bad thing it's apart of you. You need it just don't believe it.

For me I was born intuitive, I believe we all are intuitive when we are born and it's our environment belief system that will allow it to grow or not.

As I got older it was still present but not as intense but my experiences became more frequent. I had numerous déjà vu, out of body experiences and lucid dreams.

So up until 1998 for some reason I start to open up faster. Lots of coincidences and synchronistic events that I could not explain at the time.

So for 10yrs I was trying to make sense of what was happening to me I start to search for answers.

So I started my Bachelor of Arts at the age of 30 yrs in Metaphysics and with that experience I found that all the religions of the world at the root are based on LOVE and the rest is content.

So as part of my enfoldment up until now I was becoming more sensitive to the energy of my environment. I had to feel it to believe it. I couldn't take it on faith I had to experience it.

So this book is just the interpretation of my experience of my own self inquiry.

You will see it for yourself when you allow yourself to feel it so that you can believe it.

I hope you enjoyed it and if not it's just another experience.

If you need me you know where to find me I will be at the bar.

Remember you are in constant dialog with your creator. 24/7